Instant Adobe Story Starter

Develop professional scripts, ready for production

Christopher Tilford

PUBLISHING

BIRMINGHAM - MUMBAI

Instant Adobe Story Starter

First published: January 2013

Production Reference: 1160113

Published by Packt Publishing Ltd.
Livery Place
35 Livery Street
Birmingham B3 2PB, UK.

ISBN 978-1-84969-426-1

www.packtpub.com

Credits

Author

Christopher Tilford

Reviewer

Catherine Rinella

Acquisition Editor

Erol Staveley

Commissioning Editor

Priyanka Shah

Technical Editor

Dominic Pereira

Project Coordinator

Esha Thakker

Proofreader

Amy Guest

Production Coordinator

Prachali Bhiwandkar

Cover Work

Prachali Bhiwandkar

Cover Image

Conidon Miranda

About the Author

Christopher Tilford has a degree in English Literature, aside from writing and literature, Christopher has been a freelance graphic and web designer for over 6 years. He founded AzurePro Studios in 2006 as a way for him to bring life to his own creative ideas. Over the years he has met with numerous creative individuals and has developed an extensive network of talented connections.

He has a background in advertising and brings his creative flair and enthusiasm to the table. An avid creative enthusiast, he is the author of *Shattered Heaven: Sins of the Soul* and its subsequent three sequel novels. He took up screenwriting in 2007 when he began to venture into animation. With plans of producing an animated movie based on one of his novels, he found Adobe Story in 2011. Through Adobe Story, he was able to organize a full screenplay for his movie and begin the production process thanks to the tools Story had to offer. Not just a writer, he has made it his joy to become proficient in all things Adobe. From writing to graphic design and animation, Christopher has set no limits to what he would like to accomplish.

I'd like to thank my friends and family for giving me support when the opportunity to put this book together came about. There are too many to thank individually. I've been blessed with a tremendous support system, without them I wouldn't be able to do what I do.

About the Reviewer

Catherine Rinella is an audio drama producer and radio host for WCBE 90.5 FM in Columbus, Ohio. Her radio program *Midnight Audio Theatre* (http://midnightaudiotheatre.com/) regularly shares and promotes new and original audio dramas, encouraging writers, sound, and voice artists in the performance craft. She is currently working with Columbus Public School students to encourage and develop sound design skills in their Recording Arts program, and is in the process of writing and producing the second season of her own audio drama, Dreamcatcher (http://www.dreamcatcheraudio.com/).

Outside of audio drama, Catherine is a certified Audio Engineer. Graduating with two Bachelors of Music from the Ohio State University, she went on to complete her technical training with The Recording Workshop. She currently resides in Columbus, Ohio, where she runs and designs sound for multiple theater companies, works as a freelance voice actress for local production studios, and drinks an unhealthy amount of coffee.

A big thank you to Christopher for including me in this process; and to my mother, the best editor and critique I know.

www.packtpub.com

Support files, eBooks, discount offers and more

You might want to visit www.PacktPub.com for support files and downloads related to your book.

Did you know that Packt offers eBook versions of every book published, with PDF and ePub files available? You can upgrade to the eBook version at www.PacktPub.com and as a print book customer, you are entitled to a discount on the eBook copy. Get in touch with us at service@packtpub.com for more details.

At www.PacktPub.com, you can also read a collection of free technical articles, sign up for a range of free newsletters, and receive exclusive discounts and offers on Packt books and eBooks.

packtLib.packtpub.com

Do you need instant solutions to your IT questions? PacktLib is Packt's online digital book library. Here, you can access, read and search across Packt's entire library of books.

Why Subscribe?

- ✦ Fully searchable across every book published by Packt
- ✦ Copy and paste, print and bookmark content
- ✦ On demand and accessible via web browser

Free Access for Packt account holders

If you have an account with Packt at www.PacktPub.com, you can use this to access PacktLib today and view nine entirely free books. Simply use your login credentials for immediate access.

Table of Contents

Instant Adobe Story Starter

Welcome to the *Instant Adobe Story Starter*. This book has been developed specifically with new users in mind. You will learn the basics of Adobe Story and discover many of its useful and most beneficial features.

This document contains the following sections:

So, what is Adobe Story? – discover Adobe Story, see what differentiates it from word processing software and learn just what you can do with it.

Installation – learn how to set up Adobe Story with no problems, so that you can start script-writing in no time.

Quick start – in this section, you will learn how to become familiar with Adobe Story, its layout, and how to create projects and documents.

Top features you want to know about – here, you will learn some of the most beneficial features that Adobe Story has to offer. Learn about collaborating with other users, track changes in documents, and be introduced to the integration abilities with other Adobe software.

People and places you should get to know – the Adobe Story community is growing, but there's already a good amount of information to be found. This section connects you to other useful places like forums, Twitter feeds, blogs and more that will help you become more comfortable with Adobe Story.

So, what is Adobe Story?

If you installed Adobe Creative Suite 5.5 onto your computer, then you may have noticed the software **Adobe Story**. Story is an online/offline screen-writing software targeted at writers looking for better ways to keep their scripts and/or projects organized. When it was originally introduced it was a free-to-use software, readily available on Adobe's main website. It allowed the user to log in to the program while signing in with their free Adobe ID. Currently, Adobe Story is available in two different versions, a free version where you can utilize the screenwriting program through Adobe's website or Adobe Story Plus, a subscription-based version where all of its features are unlocked. With the advent of "cloud" technology (where the user entrusts their data and software over a network instead of a hard drive) and more operating systems and developers emphasizing the ability to work seamlessly through the Internet, unhindered by the restraints of a physical hard drive, Adobe Story looked to grab the interest of scriptwriters by offering them a program that would allow them to work on their scripts at home, and while away from their main computer. The ability to access Adobe Story from any computer and pick up where you left off was one of the many attractions Adobe brought about through Story.

Adobe Story also introduced the ability to share your scripts with other Adobe ID users. This is perfect when you are collaborating with multiple editors and reviewers on the same project. Provided they have an Adobe ID account, they would be able to view and edit (depending on the role you assign to them; more on that later) the documents in the project that the team would be working on. Through Adobe Story, a team of individuals are able to share documents without the hassle of e-mail. Editors and reviewers have the ability to make adjustments to the document in question just by logging into their account on either their desktop version of the program or the online version.

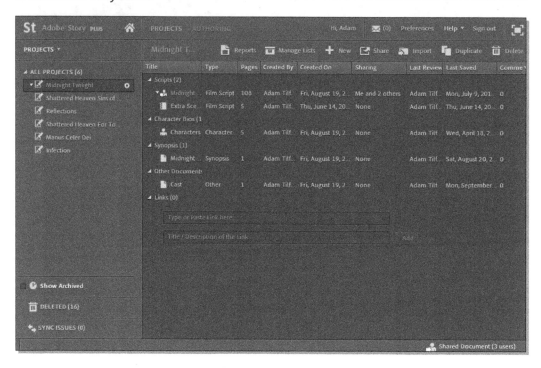

Scriptwriting is an art form that those unfamiliar with may have trouble getting started. For those just starting out, with no help or guidance, it may come across as an intimidating task to take on. Adobe Story is a program designed to help guide those who may be talented writers but are unsure of how to approach developing a script using the accepted standard. Scripts in Adobe Story are already set with the default font used in the profession and with each new paragraph, gives the writer the option of choosing the proper format based on what they are about to enter (dialog, an action shot, scene transition, and so on). Story removes the concern that plagues most writers' minds when they are attempting to create a script. No more worries about proper indentation or spacing, the program takes care of it automatically.

Adobe Story is a streamlined, shareable screenwriting program geared towards amateurs and professionals alike. It allows the user to develop professional-looking scripts, while keeping everything for a particular project organized and easily accessible.

Installation

Installation of this software is also simple and does not take much longer than a minute.

Step 1 – Choosing your version

Story is available in two forms, a free version and a subscription version. The monthly plan for Adobe Story is US $9.99.

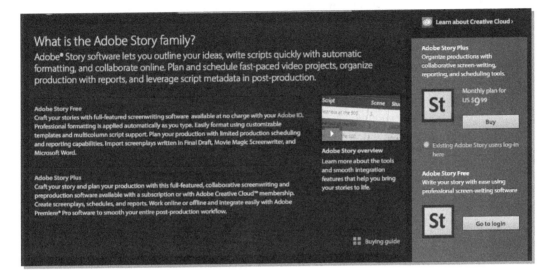

The free version of Adobe Story is a professional screenwriting software that places an emphasis on working on the go. The program gives you access to basic word processing software that is built around professional screenwriting templates. If you upgrade to the Plus version, you will be given access to a more in-depth organizational system, the ability to work on your projects both online and offline through the use of a desktop application, character auto-fill, image import, change tracking, task assignment and breakdown reports, and be allowed to share documents with other users for better collaborations.

Step 2 – Setting up your system

Following are the minimum system requirements for running Adobe Story on your computer. These are the optimum settings for Story to run smoothly:

Windows	Mac OS
✦ 1GHz or faster processor.	✦ 1GHz or faster processor.
✦ Microsoft® Windows® XP with Service Pack 3 or Windows 7.	✦ Mac OS X v10.6.8 or v10.7.
✦ 512 MB of RAM recommended.	✦ 512 MB of RAM recommended.
✦ SVGA 1280 x 768 display.	✦ SVGA 1280 x 768 display.
✦ Microsoft Internet Explorer 8 or 9, Firefox 9 or 10, or Chrome 16.	✦ Apple Safari 5, Firefox 9 or 10, or Chrome 16.
✦ 512 Kbps or faster Internet connection required.	✦ 512 Kbps or faster Internet connection required.
✦ Browser SSL support, JavaScript support, and cookies must be enabled.	✦ Browser SSL support, JavaScript support, and cookies must be enabled.
✦ Adobe® Flash® Player 10.1 software required. This software will not operate without activation. Broadband Internet connection and registration are required for software activation, validation of subscriptions, and access to online services. Note, phone activation is not available.	✦ Adobe Flash Player 10.1 software required. This software will not operate without activation. Broadband Internet connection and registration are required for software activation, validation of subscriptions, and access to online services. Note, phone activation is not available.

Step 3 – Setting up Adobe Story

The steps to set up Adobe Story are explored in the following sections.

Creating Adobe ID

First, you must establish an Adobe ID before you can proceed any further. Adobe IDs are free to create. When you are on the main page for Adobe Story — `https://story.adobe.com/en-us/index.html`, you will see the **Create Free Account** option.

Follow the steps to finish this process; the **Create an Adobe ID** dialog box is shown in the following screenshot:

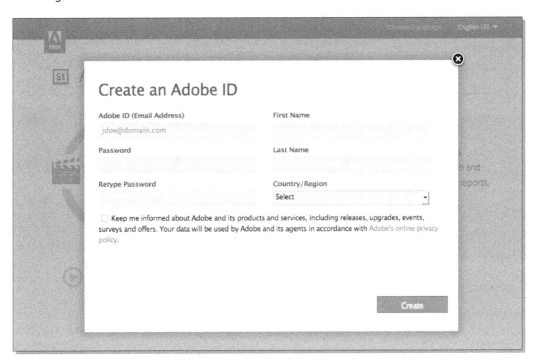

Opening Adobe Story

Once your Adobe ID is created and you verify your e-mail account, Adobe Story (free version) will become available for you to sign in. On the top-right corner of the Adobe Story screen you will see the **Upgrade Now** option. Click this button if you choose to use Adobe Story Plus. Otherwise your installation journey ends here. This button is shown in the following screenshot:

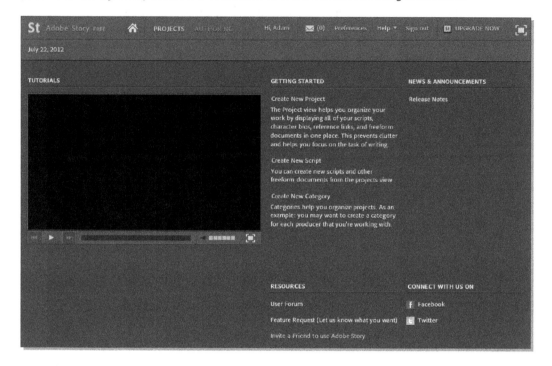

Installing desktop application

If you choose to upgrade to Plus, your home screen in the online version of Adobe Story will have a new link. On the right-half of the screen next to the Story logo, you will see the **Install Desktop Application** button. This is where you go in order to set up Adobe Story on your home computer; this button can be seen in the following screenshot:

A prompt will appear asking you if it is ok to go ahead with the installation; as shown here:

You can either choose to save the file and install it later or open it directly; these options are shown in this screenshot:

Once you choose to open the file, you will be asked to choose the location of where you want Story to be installed. For Macs, the default will be **Applications** and for Windows, `Program Files`. Refer to the following screenshot:

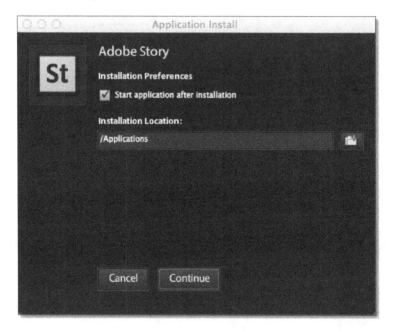

And that's it!!

The installation process is quick and shouldn't take more than a minute. Once it completes, Adobe Story Plus will open on your computer, prompting you to sign in with your Adobe ID.

Once you sign in, you will be ready to start writing your script!

Quick Start – Creating your first Adobe Story project

Adobe Story has a variety of tools that make it much more than a simple script writing program. Story is considered to be a production management program. Not only will it allow you to develop all sorts of screenplays, but it will give you the necessary tools to keep track of your entire project. We will go through the basics of Adobe Story so that you can jump right into putting your project together. We will touch on the layout of Story, how to create a document, and even the key terminology used in the industry today, as well as other vital information!

Step 1 – Getting started with the layout

Now that you are set up and ready to move forward with Adobe Story, we can look at the layout offered by Adobe. When you initially sign into the program, you are greeted with the home page. Adobe offers video tutorials and any news in regards to Story, as shown here:

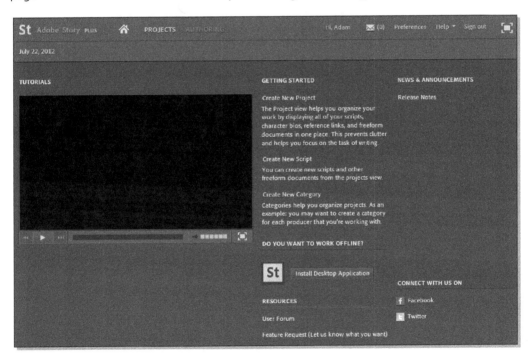

On the top bar are your options in how you would like to proceed. Next to your name is an envelope icon which holds all your notifications. If you are working with editors and reviewers, any action performed on a project that they may take will be shown to you via the notification system. It's a simple way to keep everyone working on the same script informed and up-to-date.

Step 2 – Setting your preferences

Through the **Preferences** option you are able to set up beneficial features such as **Auto Save, Notifications, Back up/Restore, Script Editor,** and **Schedule**; as shown in the following screenshot:

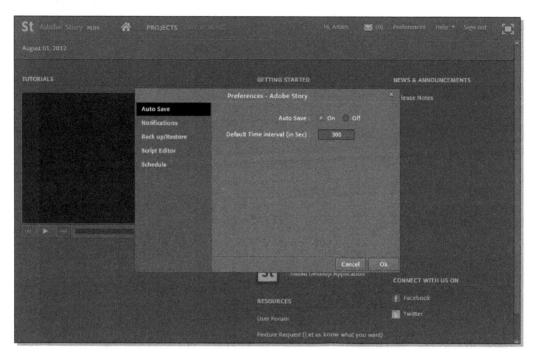

Auto Save

Either turn it on or off. When it is on, you can control how often Story saves your document. It is recommended to keep this enabled, you never know when something may happen to cause you to lose work that hasn't been saved.

Notifications

Simply choose if you wish to have all updates sent directly to your e-mail.

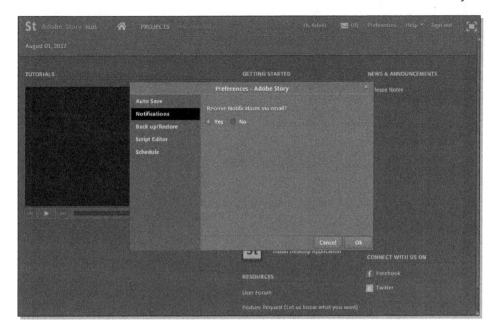

Back up/Restore (for Adobe Story Plus users only)

Available only for Adobe Story Plus (categories, projects, scripts, and so on) onto a FTP or SFTP server, providing you have the required permissions that server may require. If needed, you will be able to use the backup file that is created on the server to restore all data.

If you have access to a web server, Adobe Story allows you to connect to it through either an FTP or SFTP connection. Story will send backups of your documents to the server just in case something may go wrong.

The different parameters that need to be filled in—also shown in the previous screenshot—are explained as follows:

✦ **Host name**: Usually is the domain name connected to the FTP account. For example, `shatteredheaven.com`.

✦ **Directory**: Only relevant if you have a specific folder you would like to send the backups to. For example, `/backup`.

✦ **User name**: The username you use to access your FTP server.

Along with the documents backed up, all of their organizational information is saved as well. Everything will be restored to its original location.

A notification will appear after every backup or restore operation that occurs. The success or failure of this process will be displayed in the notification.

The steps to set up the **Back up** or the **Restore** option are as follows:

1. In the **Projects** view, click **Projects.**

2. Select the **Back up/Restore** options, as shown in the following screenshot:

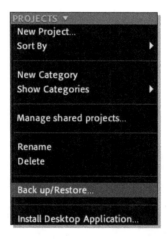

3. In the **Back up/Restore** account data, fill in your information.

4. Select either the **Back up** or **Restore** option.
    - To back up projects, select **Back up**
    - To restore a project that has already been backed up, select **Restore**

5. Enter the address for the server that you either intend to back up the projects to, or that has the recovery data of a previously backed up project.

6. Specify the location of the directory on the server (optional).

7. If you are creating a backup, you can choose to change the default name of the backup file. The default backup name is `your first name_Date of initiation of the backup_Time of initiation of the backup`. When restoring data, enter the name of the backup file to restore.

8. Enter your login details for the server.

9. Select the connection type, FTP or SFTP.

10. Click **Ok** to back up or restore data.

Script Editor

The **Script Editor** option allows you to control the layout when editing a document.

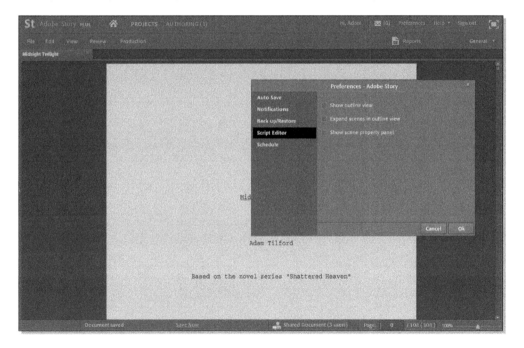

The previous screenshot is an example without any of the options enabled.

The same script, but with the **Show outline view** checkbox enabled is shown in the following screenshot.

The outline view creates a column on the left-hand side of the screen which lists all of the **Scenes** within the full script. By double-clicking on a specific scene, you will be brought to that exact location in the script (shown in the following screenshot). It makes editing much more organized and easier to access.

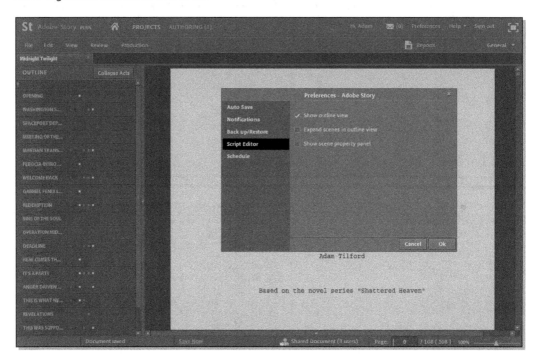

We have now enabled the **Expand scenes in outline view** checkbox. By turning this feature on, you are able to preview the content of each individual scene in the outline column. A new scrollbar appears on the far left-hand side, allowing you to scroll through the entire scene without having to move from your current position in the script.

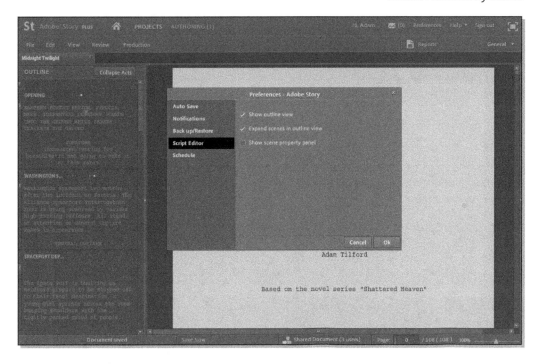

Schedule

You can either choose to utilize the **Use Start of Day Breaks** option, which points out the start of a day's worth of shooting for visual projects, or the **Use End of Day Break** option, which marks the end of a day's worth of shooting. These options are used for noting how much work you intend to cover during that day. These are not for lunch breaks within a full scheduled day of work.

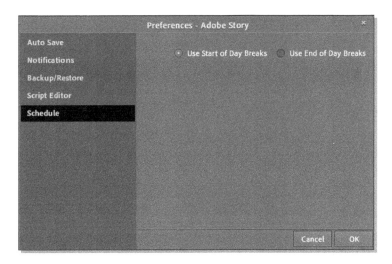

Step 3 – Getting started

With your preferences set you are ready to create a project! When you click the **Projects** tab, located next to the icon of a house, you will be brought to the following screen. This screen is known as the **Projects View**.

There are three different views in Adobe Story: Home, **PROJECTS**, and **AUTHORING**.

Home

The following screen is what is considered the Home screen, it is the initial screen that you are greeted with upon logging into Adobe Story. From here you can view video tutorials and access community resources:

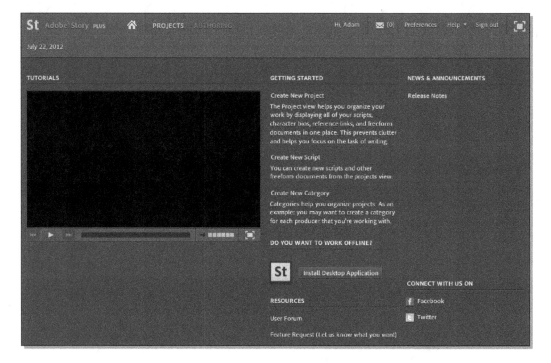

PROJECTS

The **PROJECTS** screen is shown in the following screenshot. This serves as the outline home for all of your created projects. Here you can access and create documents that are integral to your overall project:

AUTHORING

The **AUTHORING** view, as shown here, is where all the content for a script is created. Think of it as the word processor portion of Adobe Story.

Navigating between views

In the following screenshot, you can see the icons for each of the different view points shown previously:

In order to travel between the three different viewing options, refer to the menu bar on the upper-left corner of the screen. **AUTHORING** is initially disabled. In order to enable it, when you're in the **PROJECTS** view, double-click on a script in order to bring up the **AUTHORING** view. When a script is open, a number will appear in a parenthesis next to **AUTHORING**. The number will change depending on the amount of scripts that are currently open.

The PROJECTS view

When you're in the **PROJECTS** view, you can perform the following tasks.

+ Create new projects
+ Add new scripts
+ Import scripts into projects
+ Add scripts to projects
+ Add projects to categories
+ Add other documents, such as character biographies, synopsis, pitch, or other to a project
+ Add links that you frequently utilize
+ Get information about a script and who it may be shared with

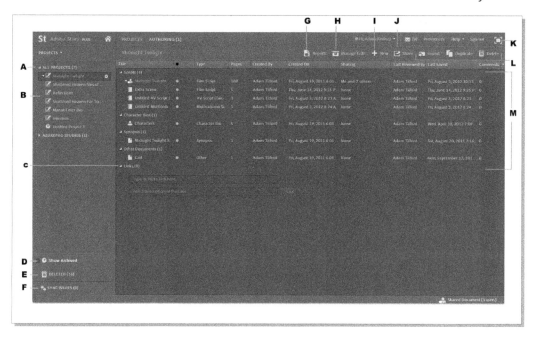

Refer to the preceding screenshot and follow the explanation given in the following table:

Identification	Description
A	The **PROJECTS** menu
B	List of projects
C	Option to add links
D	Option to view archived projects
E	Deleted items
F	Sync issues
G	Generate production reports
H	Manage lists
I	Create new document
J	Add sharing to a document
K	Toggle full screen
L	Import, duplicate, and delete
M	Information columns showing information on specific documents

Customizing the columns

You have the option to customize the columns that are displayed. On the right-hand side of the screen, after the last column, there is an arrow. Click the arrow and a checklist relating to all the columns appear. You can choose to toggle on/off which ever information you may or may not want to view when in the **PROJECTS** view. This is shown here:

Adding frequently-used links

If you are jumping back and forth between various links that are useful, Adobe Story allows you to insert them into Story by using the option shown in the following screenshot:

This is located on the bottom-right panel in the **PROJECTS** view.

The AUTHORING view

The **AUTHORING** view is disabled by default. In order to open it, open a script/document from the **PROJECTS** view.

When you're in the **AUTHORING** view, you can perform the following tasks:

✦ Create, edit, review, and share scripts/documents

✦ Create shooting scripts

✦ Tag scripts

+ Import and export scripts in different formats, such as PDF, Txt, CSV, and FDX SEX
+ Print scripts
+ Generate breakdown reports (Adobe Plus)

Refer to the preceding screenshot and follow the explanation given in the following table to better understand this view:

Identification	Description
A	Menu bar
B	Tabbed script panel
C	Scene outline panel
D	Colored dots that indicate certain character elements
E	Find options
F	Scene properties panel
G	Link to access recently shared scripts
H	Reports
I	Comments

Identification	Description
J	Toggle Full screen
K	Scene elements
L	Tagging pane
M	Editing panel

The Scene property panel

The scene properties panel can be accessed when you're in the **AUTHORING** view. When you enable the **Show scene property panel** checkbox, a new column appears on the right-hand side of the screen. When you select a scene from the outline column, all of its information will appear in the property column. Adobe Story gives you a wide variety of options to help organize each scene to the best of your ability.

You can view the **SCENE PROPERTIES**, **COMMENTS**, and **TAGS** options when you enable this checkbox.

SCENE PROPERTIES

The **SCENE PROPERTIES** option is shown in the following screenshot:

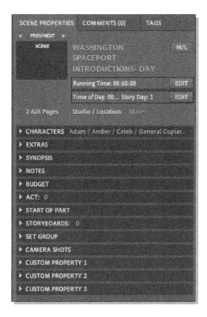

You can manually choose the time or Story will automatically set it.

In the previous screenshot, **Running Time** is selected. Auto set is based on the page length, going by the assumption of a single page equals 1 minute of play.

You can also set the time of day in which the scene takes place by using the **Time of Day** field shown in the following screenshot:

This panel contains the following features or options:

Option	Description
CHARACTERS	Lists all the characters that have dialog in the current scene, as well as detects and lists all non-speaking characters
EXTRAS	Lists any and all "extra" roles that are in the scene
SYNOPSIS	A brief summary of the events that take place in the scene
NOTES	Any notes you may have for the scene
BUDGET	The finances set for the scene
ACT	Shows any acts that you may have set up for the scene
START OF PART	Relates to the act in the scene
STORYBOARDS	Shows any drawn up storyboards that you may have for the specific scene
SET GROUP	Any groups connected to the script will appear here
CAMERA SHOTS	All designated camera shots will be listed
CUSTOM PROPERTIES	This is just an open area where you can put any other scene notes or information that do not fit anywhere specific

Creating new projects

All documents and scripts are contained within the specific projects that you create. This is similar to folders on your computer. Before beginning, you must create a new project, otherwise, any and all documents and scripts you create will be held in the sample projects section that comes as default with Adobe Story. You can create new projects in two ways.

The first being from the home screen under **GETTING STARTED**; as shown here:

On the left-hand side of the screen, you can create a new project from the **PROJECTS** work screen, as shown in this screenshot:

You are taken directly to your new project once it is created. When naming a project, do not include any special characters. The following screen will display when a new project is created:

Renaming projects

If at a later date you wish to change the name of your project, you are able to do that as well; here are the steps:

1. Select the project in the **PROJECTS** view.

2. Click the arrow to the left of the project

3. Select **Rename**; as shown here:

4. Enter the new name

Filling in the production information

You can adjust the specific information in regards to your project as well. There is a gear-like icon on the right-hand side of your highlighted project; this is only available in Story Plus.

When this icon is clicked, the following window is opened, where we can fill in all our production information:

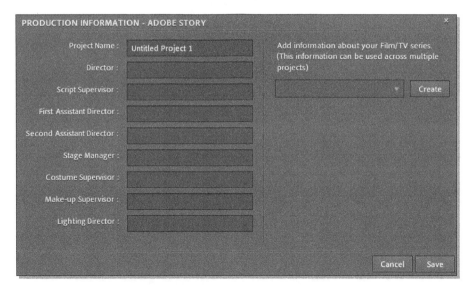

Deleting and restoring deleted documents

Once you delete a project, it is removed permanently. However, all of its contents are then placed in the **DELETED** section.

Once you delete contents within the **DELETED** section, they are removed forever.

After deleting a project, you may wish to restore those contents and move them to a newer one. But you must create a new project with the same name as the one that was originally deleted. Follow these steps to restore a project:

1. In the **PROJECT** view, click **DELETED** on the left-hand side panel.

2. Select the document you wish to restore.

3. Click the arrow to the left of the document.

4. Select **Restore To Project**

5. Select the project you wish to restore the document to.

Step 4 – Categories

You can efficiently organize your documents and projects when using categories. If certain clients have multiple projects running, you can place all of those projects into a specific category to keep them from being mixed in with any other projects.

Create a new category

To create a new category, in the **PROJECTS** view, select **Projects | New Category** and enter the name for the category.

Adding projects to categories

To add projects to the category, you can simply drag the project from the project menu to the category you wish to add it to as shown here:

Renaming a category

Select **Projects | Rename**, press *F2*, or double-click the category.

Removing projects from categories

Follows these steps to remove projects from categories:

1. Select the project that you want to remove.
2. Click the arrow on the left.
3. Select **Remove From Category**.

Deleting a category

To delete a category:

1. Select the category that you want to delete.
2. Select **Projects | Delete**.

Step 5 – Archiving a project

Archive projects are typically ones that are not used frequently and therefore do not need to be present in view. All projects that are archived are hidden from view. Select the project in the **PROJECTS** view, click the arrow on the left-hand side and select **Archive**. If you want to view what you have archived, on the left-bottom corner of the screen you will see a clock icon and next to it will be the words **Show Archived**; select this.

If you want to restore an archived project, make sure the **Show Archived** option is selected and then select the project. Click the arrow to the left of the project to bring up a drop-down menu and select **Restore**.

Step 6 – Creating scripts and documents

Before you begin, you should be aware of the different types of documents you are able to create in Adobe Story. These are as follows:

+ **Film Script**: Standard industry screenplay format for film

+ **TV Script**: Standard industry screenplay format for TV

+ **AV Script**: A two-column script for audio and video correspondence

+ **Multicolumn Script**: A three-column script that includes **Shot Number Visual,** and **Audio**

+ **Character Bio**: Character information

+ **Schedule**: Outline your schedule

+ **Logline**: A brief summary of a program that usually provides both the synopsis and some sort of emotional hook to gain interest

+ **Pitch**: The short description of your project that would gain interest

+ **Research**: Collect all of your project research

+ **Summary**: Similar to a synopsis, it serves as a condensed version of the story

+ **Synopsis**: A brief summary of the major points of a project

+ **Other**: Use for whatever else you may think of, that doesn't fit in with the other options

To create a new document, simply click the **New** icon, and the following menu will be brought up:

All scripts in Adobe Story contain the industry standard formatting to provide assistance. Each element within the script automatically is applied by the format of the script chosen to create. In addition to this, you are also able to create Free Form documents, documents that are not bound to specific types of formatting.

Scenes

Scenes are subdivisions of a screenplay/script. An individual scene describes a series of actions set to a specific location, time, and characters involved. Breaking a single script into multiple scenes is necessary to keep proper organization for the overall project.

Scene Elements

There are standard "elements" that are used when it comes to script writing; these are:

Element	Description
Scene heading	This element usually opens the scene. For example, INT/EXT. <NAME OF THE LOCATION> - <TIME OF DAY>.
Action	Is an introduction to the scene, or any action that is being described.
Character	The name of the character involved in the action, or speaking the dialog.
Parenthetical	The tone/direction the actor uses when speaking the dialogue. For example, sarcastic, upset, angry, and so on.
Dialog	The character's dialog.
Transition	This indicates the end of the scene.
General	This element is for use if the text you are writing does not fit any of the other classifications.

Script outline

The **OUTLINE** panel on the right-hand side in the **AUTHORING** view displays all of the different scenes in the entire script. The scene heading represents the scene in the script and when you click on the heading, the contents of that particular scene will be displayed below. You are able to copy content from the outline to the main editing panel.

Whenever you complete a scene, it is added to this panel without any additional work from you. If you wish to go to a specific scene in the script, you can simply double-click the desired scene in the **OUTLINE** view and the editor will jump to the required area in the document.

It is also possible to reorder scenes by dragging a header title and moving it to a desired location.

If you want to delete a scene, you can just click the **X** icon for that scene in this view.

The colored dots shown after the header represent the characters that participate in that scene. The six most frequently appearing characters in the script are listed here. The first dot represents the character that appears the most across all the scenes. If you want to display the name of the character the dot represents, just move your cursor over the dot. The **OUTLINE** panel is shown here:

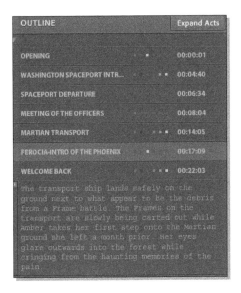

Navigating scenes

In Adobe Story, moving between scenes is simple and can be done without having to scroll through the entire document just to arrive at your desired destination. Here are the steps to navigate to and fro among the scenes:

1. Select **Edit | Jump | Next Scene**.
2. Select **Edit | Jump | Prev Scene**.

Utilizing scene elements

In normal word processors, you would have to set up the margins and layout based on the industry-standard format, manually. In Adobe Story, the program does it for you. In order to implement a particular element of a script, all you have to do is hit *Enter* to move to the next line and a small window will appear on the editor, like so:

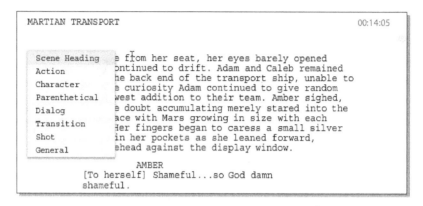

From here you can choose which element you would like to use. When you do, the document will automatically format it to the correct position.

You can also choose an element manually from the drop-down menu on the upper-right corner of the editor; as shown in the following screenshot:

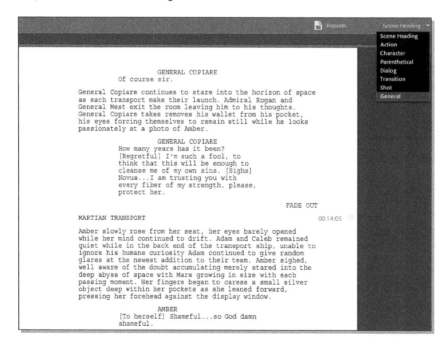

In the following screenshot, a sample scene is shown where some elements are used:

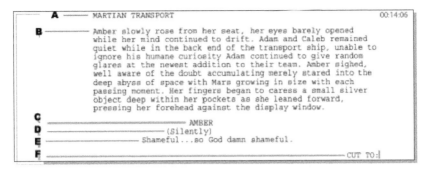

Refer to the following table where the elements used in the previous screenshot are described:

Identification	Element
A	Scene heading
B	Action
C	Character
D	Parenthetical
E	Dialog
F	Transition

Navigating among scene elements

Similar to how you can jump between scenes in a script, you are able to jump between elements. Follow these steps to do so:

1. Select **Edit | Jump | Next Element** to move to the next scene element of the same type in the document. Shortcut: *Ctrl/Cmd + J*.

2. Select **Edit | Jump | Prev Element** to move to the previous scene element of the same type in the document. Shortcut: *Ctrl/Cmd+ K*.

Storyboards

Storyboards are drawn representations of how scenes play out. They are the outline for visual direction, working alongside the script to produce the desired result.

You can view and manage storyboards from the **Scene Properties** panel. You can add one or more storyboard images for each individual scene.

Adding storyboard images

Follow these steps to add storyboard images:

1. In the **Scene Properties** panel, under the **Storyboard** button, click **Add Image Link** inside the square placeholder.

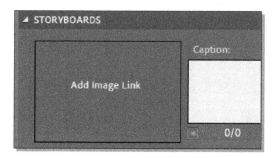

2. Or, you can also select a string of text or scene that you would like to add storyboard images to. Right-click and select **Storyboard**. The **Manage Images** dialog appears with the selected text string added as the caption.

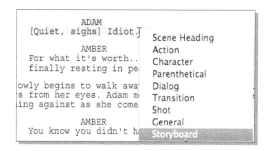

3. In the **Manage Image** dialog, click **Add Image Link** and paste a link from an online image and click **OK**.

4. You can type in a caption for the storyboard if there is no specific string of text already attached.

5. To add more images, simply click **Add Image Link** at the bottom of the **Manage Images** dialog.

With all of this, you are ready to begin creating scripts and other sorts of documents using Adobe Story. But it is only a small part of what Adobe Story has to offer; there are many features that the program is prepared with, all of which to create a more effective and organized project for you to work with. We've discussed the three different view setups, how to prepare your own preferences, making projects and categories, and how to start making industry-standard scripts that utilize elements.

Top features you'll want to know about

Adobe Story has a variety of features that have been built in for your script writing convenience. There are seven features that can be considered more helpful than others. Knowledge of these will streamline your script writing process with the overall production of a project. It is vital to be aware of them.

1 – Track changes and production revisions (for Adobe Story Plus only)

It is important to keep track of any changes you or someone else may make to a document. It's easy to save over the previous version with the new one, but what if you want to compare the previous and current versions to one another? You are able to track any and all revisions through this feature. Called revision styles, all revisions become associated with a unique style for easier identification.

Track changes

Before moving to revisions, we need to be able to know how to insert and track changes made to a document. This is how it is done:

1. When in the **AUTHORING** view, in the document, go to the **Review** tab in the top tool bar. Check **Start Tracking Changes** to enable it, and uncheck it to disable:

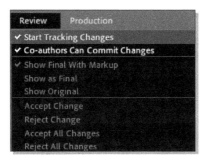

2. When it is checked, any new content you add will be in red text and highlighted:

```
                    KAREN
        I'm guessing you wanted to talk
        about Anne again? [Sighs] We
        already know about the issue. She
        has to handle things by hereself.
```

3. There is a speech bubble on the right-hand side of the addition, which allows for the person making the change to add a comment. Click on the icon to open the comment window:

4. When you place the cursor over the inserted change, a new bubble will appear telling you who made the change and when. On the far right-hand side, you can either accept or reject the change:

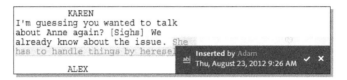

Production revisions

You have to be in the Authoring view in order to make a revision. Production revisions highlight certain pages where changes have been made. The script becomes locked and all changes are highlighted in the revision style you choose. On the title page, a note is inserted on the bottom-right corner giving the date of the last revision. This is also done on the footer of every page where there is a change. The color changes and borders will not be exported in a PDF.

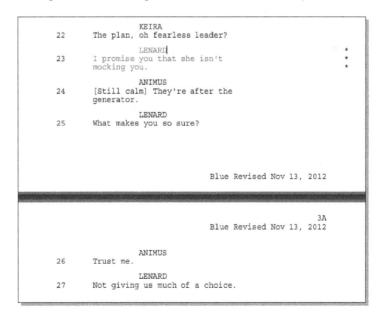

Before starting a revision, make sure that you have done the following:

1. Act on all tracked changes in your document by accepting or rejecting them.
2. Disable track changes after completing accepting/rejecting tracked changes.

Now, after completing the preceding steps, follow these steps:

1. Select **Production | Start Revision**.

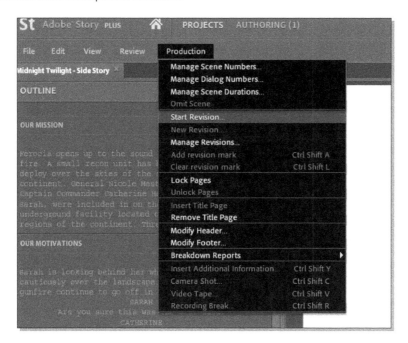

2. In the **Active Revision** drop-down, choose a revision style:

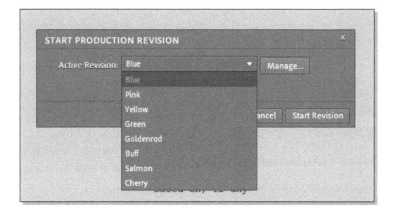

This style will be used for the markups in the revision. Make sure that you haven't already used the chosen style for a previous revision document.

3. Click **Start Revision**.

Creating a revision style

Follow these steps to create your revision style:

1. Select **Production | Manage Revisions**.

2. Click on the **+** icon.

3. Enter a name for the style

4. The following options can be tailored according to your needs:

   ○ **Revision Color**: Used to choose a color from the color menu. This color will then be applied to all the revised text and the border of the individual pages that contain the revisions. The border color will not be displayed in a printed or exported document.

   ○ **Mark**: The default mark is displayed on the right of the revised content. You can change this mark by choosing any symbol of your liking.

   ○ **Date**: The revision date.

   ○ **Revision Text Style**: The chosen formatting option is used to display revised text.

5. Click **Done** and your new style will be available from now on.

Deleting or modifying existing revisions

Let's take a look at how we can delete or modify already existing revisions:

1. Select the style that you want to delete or modify.

2. You can do either of the following:

   ○ Click on the **-** sign to delete the style

   ○ To modify, simply edit its values and click **Done**

Display options for revisions

Adobe Story also provides some display options for revisions, here's how we can set them up:

1. Select **Production | Manage Revisions**.

2. In **Viewing Options,** the following display options can be personalized according to your needs:

   ° **Show Markup For**: The options are **Select All** or **Active**. This will let you choose whether you want to have all the markups shown for all revisions or just the active ones.

   ° **Mark Position**: The mark you set in **Revision Style** is set to the right-hand side by default; you can also change its position.

   ° **Show Date In Script Header and Footer**: If you do not want to display the date, disable this option.

Locking or unlocking scene numbers

When you lock scene numbers, you prevent the renumbering of existing scenes whenever a new scene is added during production revisions.

When you do insert a new scene, Adobe Story will apply a number to the scene preceding it. For example, if you add a new scene in between scene 4 and 5, it will be numbered 4A. Here's how we can lock and unlock scene numbers:

1. Select **Production | Manage Scene Numbers**.

2. Select the **Keep Existing Scene Number** option to lock all current scenes. To unlock, deselect **Keep Existing Scene Number**.

Omitting or unomitting scenes

Adobe Story allows you to remove a scene without affecting the scene numbers remaining in the script. The word **OMITTED** will appear at the location of the scene you've chosen to omit. You can, at a later date, unomit the scene if you chose and recover the content.

To omit a scene, simply place your cursor on the scene and then select **Production | Omit Scene**. To unomit a scene, place your cursor on the omitted scene and then select **Production | Unomit Scene**.

Printing production revisions

If you want to print your revisions, it is easy to do so; just follow these steps:

1. Select **File | Print**.

2. Choose any one of the following option:

   ° **Entire Script**
   ° **All ChangedPages**
   ° **Revision**

3. To print in color, select the **Print Revised Text In Color** option.

Identifying the total number of revised pages

Here's how we can identify the total number of revised pages:

1. Select **Production | Manage Revisions**.

2. In **Viewing Options**, select **All** and click **Done**.

2 – Tagging

Along with the advent of the "cloud" concept, tagging individual words to content has become something of a norm in today's online society. Adobe Story has incorporated a similar system. With tagging, you can tag words and phrases in your scripts automatically, or manually by using the **Tagging Panel** option. For example, "boom" can be tagged as "sound effect".

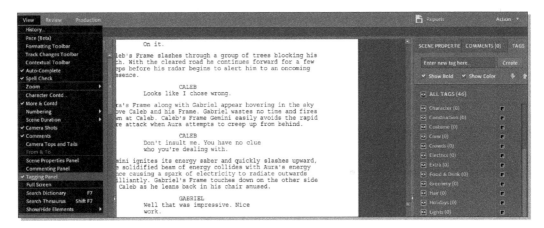

Tagging panel

1. To open the panel, you must be first in the **AUTHORING** view.

2. Select **View | Tagging Panel**.

3. The panel will open on the right-hand side of the document.

4. To add tags to the panel, enter the name of the tag in the field next to the **Create** button:

5. To delete a tag from the tagging panel, select the tag and then click on the **Delete this Tag** link:

Tagging automatically

You must be in the online mode for the **Autotagging** feature to work. It will not work in the offline mode.

 The **Autotagging** feature is only available for English scripts.

This is how it's done:

1. Select **File | Tagging | Start Autotagging**. Or select it from the drop-down menu option in the **Tagging** panel:

Once you enable **Autotagging**, the script will be locked. You will have to wait until the process has completed before being able to edit the document; the following screenshot shows the message being displayed:

Tagging manually

1. Select **View | Tagging Panel**.

2. Choose the word or phrase you would like to tag. If what you're choosing has already been tagged, it will be appended to the tag list for the word or phrase.

3. Select a tag from **Taglist** in the **Tagging** panel.

4. Do either of the following:

    ○   Select the **Show In Bold** option if you want the tagged words or phrases to be displayed in bold.

    ○   Select the **Show Color** option if you would prefer Story to display the selected color (you can choose a color for each tag with a color palette on the right-hand of the tag in the **Taglist** panel) to the tag:

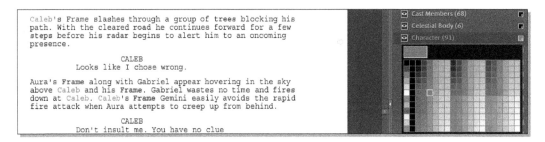

Finding words or phrases by their specific tag

Follow these steps to search for words or phrases with a specific tag:

1. Disable visibility for all tags. Enable visibility for the tag that you want to search. To do this, simply click on the eye icon on the left-hand side of the tagged word:

2. Use the arrow icons in the **Tagging** panel in order to navigate through the tags in the script. Only the visible tags will be shown.

Viewing tags associated with a word or phrase

To view tags associated with a word or a phrase, you can do either of the following:

1. Select the word/phrase. The tags associated with the word/phrase will be highlighted in the **Tagging** panel. Scroll through the panel in order to view the tags associated with it:

2. Move your mouse over the word/phrase. The information will be displayed in the tool tip:

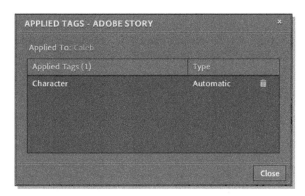

3. Hold *Ctrl* (*Cmd* on Mac) and double-click to view the associated tags:

Removing tags

1. Over the word you wish to edit, hold *Ctrl* (*Cmd* on Mac) and double-click to bring up the **Applied Tags** panel.

2. Click on the **Remove This Tag** icon for the chosen tag.

3. Click **Close**.

4. To remove all the tags, select **File | Tagging | Remove All Tags**.

5. To remove all the manual tags, select **File | Tagging | Remove All Manual Tags**.

6. To remove all the auto tags, select **File | Tagging | Remove Auto Tags**.

3 – Application for iOS-based devices

Adobe Story has an application for iOS-based devices. This application is available currently only in English. It allows you to read and review Adobe Story scripts and documents. It does not support **AV** (**Audio Visual**) scripts, Multicolumn scripts, and TV scripts as of yet.

Logging in

Before you start, make sure you have registered yourself with Adobe Story using the web or desktop application.

Use the same combination of e-mail address and password used on the full application with the iOS version. Accept the TOU before attempting to log in.

If you want to log out, select **Account** and then select **Log Out**.

Viewing documents, scene outline, and scenes

The ten most recently read files will be displayed upon logging in to the Adobe Story application.

1. To view all the documents, click **Categories**.

2. To view the scene outline, select the script in the **Recent Files** or **Categories** view.

3. To view the contents of a scene, select the scene in the scene outline. Use the arrow icons to move among the scenes.

4. To view **Notifications**, in the **Recent Files** view, select **Notifications**. A list of notifications is displayed. Highlighted notifications are for new ones.

Reviewing scripts

As long as you have author, co-author, or reviewer permissions, you will be able to review a script.

1. Open the script and navigate to the scene.

2. Do one of the following:

   ○ Double-click to select the content that you want to comment on. Click on **Comment**, or on the **Add Comment** button.

   ○ To comment on the content that has already been commented on, enter your comment in the **Write New Comment** textbox.

3. To navigate comments, use the arrow icons.

4. Click **Post**.

Viewing or deleting comments

1. In the scene containing the comments, select **Comments**.

2. The comment list is displayed. The paragraph containing the comment is highlighted when you select on a comment in the list.

3. Select **Delete** after clicking on the desired comment.

4 – Integrating with Creative Suite

Like most Adobe products, integration is integral to streamlining a full project. Adobe Story's script-to-screen workflow with Adobe Production Premium Suite CS5 and later helps turn plans into a more organized production.

All information within the script is transformed into metadata automatically upon exporting it as an ASTX file. This data helps to produce shot lists in Adobe OnLocation and in Premiere Pro; it can find relevant content, thus improving the accuracy of speech-to-text. In Encore and Media Encoder, it can be used to create searchable experiences for the audience.

What is metadata?

Metadata is something you hear about often when it comes to web design. In HTML, metadata is used to help convey proper information of content to search engines such as Google, Bing, and Yahoo. The data consists of content written in plain text that contains keywords that relate to the overall content of the page. In video production and with Adobe Story, it is more or less the same concept.

Any text content that transcripts from the script and text descriptions are utilized as metadata. These textual elements (words) are essential in the script's formatting. Scenes, characters, dialogue, actions, and so on are all identified through the use of metadata. Character names or specific actions such as "slap" are examples of metadata. If you search for the word "slap" in a program such as Premiere Pro, all scenes containing this word (element) will be brought up. This data is captured only when the script is exported as an ASTX file.

Adding metadata

Metadata can be added either automatically or manually by other software in the Adobe Production Premium suite.

Uses of metadata in the workflow

Metadata helps automate a number of time-consuming, yet important processes in the script-to-screen workflow.

Production

In the production process, you are able to use metadata for the following reasons:

✦ Manage and locate your media assets throughout the process of production. For example, when you search for the word "fight" in Premiere Pro, all the movie clips that contain the word "fight" in their metadata are displayed.

✦ You can track crucial details, such as where a clip was shot and even the actors that were in the scene.

Editing

By using metadata you can locate words in spoken dialogue using speech search in Premiere Pro. This allows you to locate and jump instantly to keywords in the spoken dialogue. This feature can only work for languages supported by Adobe Story.

Post production

In the post-production processes you can use metadata for the following:

✦ Search for clips while you edit

✦ Playback (Flash, DVD, Web-DVD, and Blu-ray)

✦ Search video content

Script-to-screen workflow

Your exported scripts from Adobe Story can be brought into Adobe OnLocation:

1. Export scripts in Adobe Story as an ASTX file.
2. Import the ASTX file into OnLocation.

OnLocation is a direct-to-disk recording, logging, and monitoring solution. The software captures all metadata information from the Adobe Story document once it is imported.

Shot lists are created automatically thanks to the imported metadata. These lists will be available in the **Project** panel.

The shot list matches the scenes in the imported Adobe Story script. Link movie clips to shot placeholders.

In OnLocation, drag a movie clip onto a shot placeholder in order to merge the Adobe Story metadata with the actual video. Adobe Story metadata is supported in the following formats:

MPEG-2 DV, MPEG-2 HDV, DVCPRO 50, DVCPRO 25, H264 DV (. mp4), XDCAM, and XDCAM EX

Importing movie clips into Premiere Pro

Metadata that has been merged with the video clips are all carried over during the import process.

The benefits from this import process help tremendously with the post-production process becoming more efficient.

Locate media assets using details such as, filename, date, time, and camera setting.

Speech Search in Premiere Pro helps search within media assets to locate and jump to keywords in spoken dialogue. The search is made more accurate due to the embedded Adobe Story script.

Metadata speeds up normally time-consuming processes. It helps to quickly locate all the clips in a project that contains a particular word.

Rough cuts can be created based on speech-analysis text in Premiere Pro. Add **In** and **Out** points directly in the **Speech Analysis** section of the **Metadata** panel. It is faster to mark **In** and **Out** points in text as opposed to doing it in the actual movie clip.

Creating video experiences for the audience

You can use Adobe Media Encoder to batch encode multiple versions of source content to a variety of video formats across various media. Media assets retain all metadata captured from Adobe Story scripts.

By using Adobe Media Encoder to create web video formats such as F4V, the metadata makes it easier for users to search its content. Users can even look for scenes that were shot at specific locations.

In Encore, the metadata can be used as the basis of DVD and Blu-ray subtitles and chapter titles. It creates a database for searching by using the metadata from speech analysis text in Premiere Pro. The interface from Web DVD will allow users to search within the DVD using keywords.

5 – Breakdown reports

This is available only in Adobe Story Plus.

When your script is completed, breakdown reports can give you a full overview of all the elements and characters required for specific scenes. Breakdown reports are generated through elements such as character, dialog, and location. These reports are all automated. Each report is exported in the standard spreadsheet format of CSV.

The types of breakdown reports that Adobe Story can generate are as follows:

Report name	Report elements
Scene	Scene number, heading, location, time of day, setting, scene duration, page number, and characters
Location	Location, scene number, shot number, setting, time of day, scene duration, shot duration, characters, and page numbers
Character	Character, scene number, heading, and dialog
Cast	Character, total dialogs, and speaking scenes
Statistics	Elements, number of occurrences (of the element), total scenes, total words, and total pages
Comments	Comment number, comment, commenter, scene number, and page number
Shot	Shot number, scene number, setting, location, shot type, camera number, camera movement, shot duration (in seconds), time of day, character, and page number
Tag	Tag occurrences, tags, page number, scene number, tagged item, and scene heading
Custom Report	Select the elements that you want listed in your report

Creating breakdown reports

Scene numbers, shot numbers, and shot duration are only displayed if they are enabled in the script.

1. Select **Production | Breakdown Reports**:

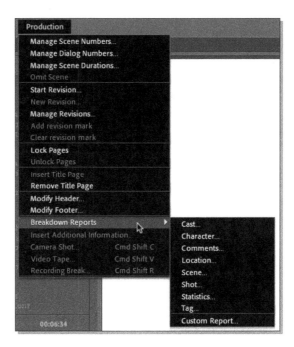

2. Select a specific report from the menu.

3. Save the report to a location on your computer.

An example of a **Statistics** breakdown report in Excel is shown here:

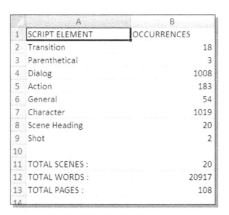

Custom breakdown reports

1. Select **Production | Breakdown Reports | Custom Report**.

2. In the dialog, select the items you want to be exported.

3. Click **Create**.

6 – Production reports

To further increase the efficiency on a project, Story gives you the option to generate reports to distribute script breakdown information with cast and crew. Unlike breakdown reports, production reports open up directly in Adobe Story.

The different types of production reports are as follows:

Type	Description
Artiste Crossplot	This lists all the sets where an artist/actor is needed across one or all the selected scripts. NA signifies that a particular scene is not assigned a studio/location. A dash (-) next to an artist's name in a scene suggests that the character is not present in the scene.
Cast Address List	It shows the cast list and their addresses.
Character Crossplot	Shows the presence of characters in scenes per script.
Colorist	It shows the day and time details for the scene in story order.
Costume Continuity	Lists the scenes in which a character is present in the script. Used for costume and makeup for production.
Running Order	Lists the script/project in story mode.
Sets and Locations	Lists the scenes based on whether it is a studio or a location shot.
Timings	This creates a table which lists scenes in story order, against, which you can enter the shooting duration details for each scene.

You can generate the following reports from a schedule:

Report type	Description
Calls	Call sheets contain schedules for actor/artists required for the production.
Camera Cards	This lists all the shots. It is in shooting order for each cameraman to shoot. If the shot number is disabled in the script, the shot will show up without a number.
Schedule Dates Crossplot	This lists the number of scenes for each actor/artist on a shooting day.
Shooting Order Script	It is a compilation of scenes in the order they were displayed in a schedule. Once this is created and sorted, you can create a script in shooting order.
Shooting Schedule	This lists all the scenes to be shot per day.
Studio Recording Order	This lists all the details of studio scenes in shooting order as well as shot information.

An example of a **Character Crossplot** production report:

Character Crossplot

Program Name: **Director:** Christopher Tilford
Program Id: **Script Supervisor:**
Episode Number: Midnight Twilight

EP/SC	TIME	DAY/ DAY NO	PAGES	SCENE
ADAM				
Midnight Twilight/2	00:00	DAY 1	(4-6)	WASHINGTON SPACEPORT INTRODUCTIONS
Midnight Twilight/5	00:00	DAY 1	(10-16)	MARTIAN TRANSPORT
Midnight Twilight/7	00:00	DAY 1	(19-24)	WELCOME BACK
Midnight Twilight/9	00:00	DAY 1	(29-40)	REDEMPTION
Midnight Twilight/11	00:00	DAY 1	(46-50)	DEADLINE
Midnight Twilight/14	00:00	DAY 1	(64-73)	ANGER DRIVEN FEELINGS RARELY FADE
Midnight Twilight/15	00:00	DAY 1	(73-85)	THIS IS WHAT NEEDS TO HAPPEN
Midnight Twilight/17	00:00	DAY 1	(88-96)	THIS WAS SUPPOSED TO BE EASY
Midnight Twilight/18	00:00	DAY 1	(96-106)	TREATY OF MARS
Midnight Twilight/19	00:00	DAY 1	(106-108)	ENDING/CREDITS

Number of Episode Scenes: 10

ADMIRAL LOWELL				
Midnight Twilight/10	00:00	DAY 1	(40-46)	OPERATION MIDNIGHT TWILIGHT
Midnight Twilight/17	00:00	DAY 1	(88-96)	THIS WAS SUPPOSED TO BE EASY

Number of Episode Scenes: 2

ADMIRAL ROGAN				
Midnight Twilight/4	00:00	DAY 1	(8-10)	MEETING OF THE OFFICERS

Number of Episode Scenes: 1

Creating a report from one or more scripts

1. In the **Projects** or the **Authoring** view, select **Reports**.

2. In the **Reports** dialog, do the following and click **Generate**.

    i. Select the type of report.

    ii. If you are doing this from the **Projects** view, select the scripts you wish to include.

    iii. To display the report, select **View report on creation**.

Creating a report from one or more scripts or a schedule

You can include the following when wanting to generate a report from multiple documents:

✦ One or more scripts for a scripting report

✦ One schedule for a scheduling report

To create a report from multiple documents do the following:

1. Select **Reports** from either in a schedule, in a script, or in the **Projects** view:

2. Select the type of report.

3. From a schedule, select **Location** or **Studio**. Select **Location** only to include the strips that have a location specified for them. Select **Studio** if you only want to include strips that are shot in a studio. Select **Location** and **Studio** to include all strips.

4. Select **View report on creation** if you want to display it.

Creating camera card reports

1. First, either in **Projects** view or in **Schedule** view, click **Reports**.

2. Specify whether you want the report to be created for all cameras or a specific one.

3. If you want to include videotape element occurrences in the report, select **Include VTs**.

4. When generating a report from the **Project** view, select **Select All Documents** or one of the schedules. A report cannot be created from more than one schedule.

Exporting reports to HTM

1. In a report, select **File | Export As | HTM – MS Word Compatible (.htm)** and save the report to your computer.

2. Right-click on the file and choose to open the file with MS Word.

7 – Scheduling

In the latest edition of Adobe Story, the feature of scheduling was added as a way to further improve the time management needed for a production.

 This is limited to only three schedules in Adobe Story Free.

Follow these steps to create a schedule:

1. In the **Projects** view, click **New**.

2. In the **Authoring** view, select **File | New**.

3. Select **Schedule** from the **Type** menu:

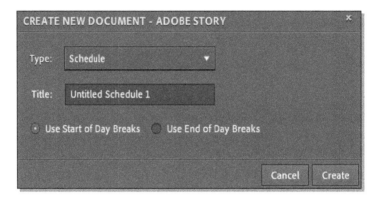

4. Give it a title and click **Create**.

5. Choose the category and project first and then select one or more scripts that you want to create the schedule with. Use *Shift* + click to select scripts in a sequence or *Ctrl* + click (*Cmd* + click in Mac) to select multiple scripts that are not in a row:

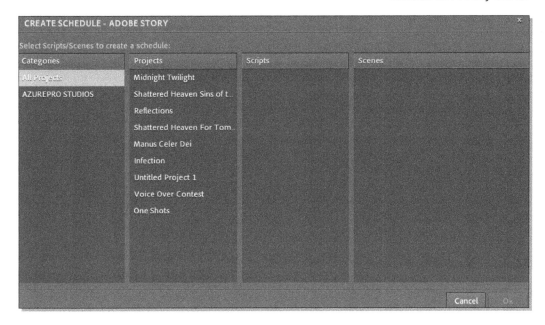

6. If you have selected a single script, then you can select the scenes that you want to schedule. If you select multiple scripts, Story will create the schedule for all the scenes in the elected scripts:

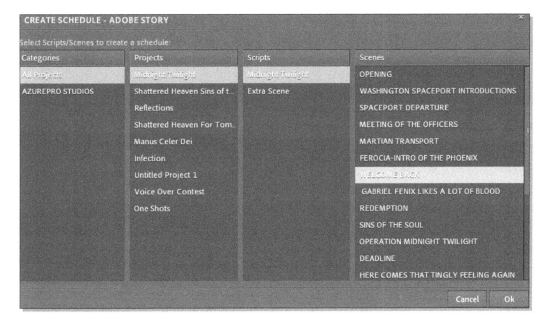

7. Click **OK** to generate the schedule.

An example of what a schedule for a script looks like in Adobe Story:

Script	Scene	Studio / Location: INT / Ext	Day / Ni	Set	Set Group	Running Tim	Pages	Story ID	Time of	Characters	Extras	Schedule Notes	Notes	S. Start	S. End
START OF DAY 1		Untitled Day Break									DATE: Friday, 24 Aug 2012		6 PAGES	FROM 00:00	TO 00:00
START OF DAY 2		Untitled Day Break									DATE: Friday, 24 Aug 2012		107 PAGES	FROM 00:00	TO 00:00
Midnight Twilight	1		DAY	OPENING		00:01:58	2 1/8	1	00:00	AMBER/ GABRIEL/ JESSICA/ JONATHAN/ NATHAN/				00:00	00:00
Midnight Twilight	2		DAY	WASHINGTON SPACEPORT INTRODUCTIONS		00:02:42	2 6/8	1	00:00	ADAM/ AMBER/ CALEB/ GENERAL COPIARE/ OFFICER 1/ OFFICER 1/ STEPHEN/ WARRANT OFFICER/				00:00	00:00
Midnight Twilight	3		DAY	SPACEPORT DEPARTURE		00:01:54	2	1	00:00	ASHLEY/ RECRUITER/ XANDER				00:00	00:00
Midnight Twilight	4		DAY	MEETING OF THE OFFICERS		00:01:30	1 5/8	1	00:00	ADMIRAL ROGAN/ GENERAL COPIARE/ GENERAL MEST/				00:00	00:00
Midnight Twilight	5		DAY	MARTIAN TRANSPORT		00:08:02	6 1/8	1	00:00	ADAM/ AMBER/ CALEB/ JONATHAN/ MARIO/ NATHAN/ STEPHEN				00:00	00:00
Midnight Twilight	6		DAY	FEROCIA-INTRO OF THE PHOENIX		00:03:18	3 3/8	1	00:00	CATHERINE/ GABRIEL/ SARAH/ VICTOR				00:00	00:00

Day breaks

You have the ability to choose to have either end-of-day breaks or start-of-day-breaks. A **day break** is what marks the end of the day or start of one in a schedule. It also displays the total number of pages in the scenes for a specific day. By doing this, you get an idea of just what you will be trying to cover in a span of a day.

A **banner** is what is referred to as any sort of break away from an end-of-day break. An example of this would be a lunch break.

Adding breaks to the schedule

In a schedule, do one of the following:

1. Select a row and click **Add Break | Day Break**. Story will insert a day break below the row that is selected.

2. Select a row and click **Add Break | Break**. A break is inserted below the selected row. Edit the title and duration of the break. The start time of the break is the same as the end time of the previous scene before.

3. Select a row and click **Break | Banner**. A banner will then be inserted below the selected row.

Start of Day Breaks and End of Day Breaks

1. From the **Projects** view, select **Preferences**.

2. In the **Preferences** box, select **Schedule**. Choose either **Use Start of Day Breaks** or **End of Day Breaks**.

Adding scenes or scripts to a schedule

1. Open the schedule.
2. Select **Edit | Add Scenes/Scripts**.
3. Select the category and the project.
4. Choose the script or scene that you want to add to the schedule.
5. Click **OK**.

Removing a script from a schedule

1. When in the schedule, select **Edit | Remove Scripts**.
2. Select one or more scripts that are to be removed.
3. Click **OK**.

If a scene is going to be split up throughout multiple days, Story gives you the option to split a scene in the schedule:

1. Right-click on a scene, from the pop-up menu, select **Split Scene**. The strip is split into two.

Automatically calculating the shooting time

When you enter the scene's start time (S. Start) and scene's duration (S. Dur) for a strip, Story calculates and shows the following:

✦ The end time of the strip (S. End)

✦ Start time and end time of the strips in the schedule until a day's break

There are many advantages of using Adobe Story as your scriptwriting software. Story does a wonderful job of pulling in all the different, varying aspects that go hand in hand with developing a project and throws them all into one program.

People and Places You Should Get to Know

If you need help with Story, here are some people and places which will prove invaluable.

Official Adobe sites

✦ **Adobe Story for iPad, iPod, and iPhone**: `https://itunes.apple.com/us/app/adobe-story/id430876855?mt=8`

✦ **Adobe Story's official website**: `https://story.adobe.com/en-us/index.html`

✦ **Adobe Creative Cloud**: `http://www.adobe.com/products/creativecloud.html?promoid=JQPEQ`

✦ **Adobe Story's help and support**: `http://help.adobe.com/en_US/story/cs/using/index.html?promoid=JTXQH`

✦ **Adobe product website**: `http://www.adobe.com/products/catalog.html`

✦ **Adobe Story's Facebook page**: `https://www.facebook.com/adobestory`

✦ **Adobe Story's community forum**: `http://forums.adobe.com/community/cslive/story`

✦ **Adobe's official blog for all Creative Suite updates**: `http://blogs.adobe.com/csupdates/`

Articles and Tutorials

✦ **Adobe tutorials**: `http://www.adobe.com/support/tutorials/`

✦ **Adobe TV**: `http://tv.adobe.com/show/adobe-story/`

✦ **AzurePro introduction to Adobe Story article**: `http://azureprostudios.com/Blog/2011/adobe-story/`

Twitter

✦ **Christopher Tilford's Twitter**: `https://twitter.com/christilford`

✦ **Adobe Story on Twitter**: `https://twitter.com/AdobeStory`

✦ **AzurePro Studios Twitter**: `https://twitter.com/AzurePro`

Blogs

✦ **Adobe Story team blog**: `http://blogs.adobe.com/story/`

✦ **AzurePro Studios**: `http://azureprostudios.com/Blog/`

Sample script

✦ **Shattered Heaven: Midnight Twilight "Our Path" Script made in Adobe Story**: `http://azureprostudios.com/Midnight%20Twilight%20-Our%20Path.pdf`

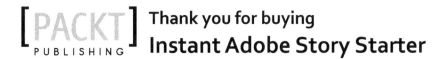

About Packt Publishing

Packt, pronounced 'packed', published its first book "*Mastering phpMyAdmin for Effective MySQL Management*" in April 2004 and subsequently continued to specialize in publishing highly focused books on specific technologies and solutions.

Our books and publications share the experiences of your fellow IT professionals in adapting and customizing today's systems, applications, and frameworks. Our solution based books give you the knowledge and power to customize the software and technologies you're using to get the job done. Packt books are more specific and less general than the IT books you have seen in the past. Our unique business model allows us to bring you more focused information, giving you more of what you need to know, and less of what you don't.

Packt is a modern, yet unique publishing company, which focuses on producing quality, cutting-edge books for communities of developers, administrators, and newbies alike. For more information, please visit our website: www.packtpub.com.

Writing for Packt

We welcome all inquiries from people who are interested in authoring. Book proposals should be sent to author@packtpub.com. If your book idea is still at an early stage and you would like to discuss it first before writing a formal book proposal, contact us; one of our commissioning editors will get in touch with you.

We're not just looking for published authors; if you have strong technical skills but no writing experience, our experienced editors can help you develop a writing career, or simply get some additional reward for your expertise.

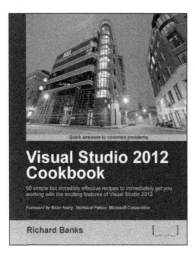

[PACKT]
PUBLISHING

Visual Studio 2012 Cookbook

ISBN: 978-1-84968-652-5   Paperback: 272 pages

50 simple but incredibly effective recipes to immediately get you working with the exciting features of Visual Studio 2012

1. Take advantage of all of the new features of Visual Studio 2012, no matter what your programming language specialty is!

2. Get to grips with Windows 8 Store App development, .NET 4.5, asynchronous coding and new team development changes in this book and e-book

3. A concise and practical First Look Cookbook to immediately get you coding with Visual Studio 2012

Microsoft SharePoint 2010 Development with Visual Studio 2010 Expert Cookbook

ISBN: 978-1-84968-458-3   Paperback: 296 pages

Develop, debug, and deploy business solutions for SharePoint applications using Studio 2010

1. Create applications using the latest client object model and create custom web services for your SharePoint environment with this book and ebook.

2. Full of illustrations, diagrams and key points for debugging and deploying your solutions securely to the SharePoint environment.

3. Recipes with step-by-step instructions with detailed explanation on how each recipe works and working code examples.

Please check **www.PacktPub.com** for information on our titles

Sony Vegas Pro 11 Beginner's Guide

ISBN: 978-1-84969-170-3   Paperback: 264 pages

Edit videos with style and ease using Vegas Pro

1. Edit slick, professional videos of all kinds with Sony Vegas Pro

2. Learn audio and video editing from scratch

3. Speed up your editing workflow

4. A practical beginner's guide with a fast-paced but friendly and engaging approach towards video editing

Microsoft Dynamics CRM 2011: Dashboards Cookbook

ISBN: 978-1-84968-440-8   Paperback: 266 pages

Over 50 simple but incredibly effective recipes for creating, customizing, and interacting with rich dashboards and charts

1. Explore the Processing language with a broad range of practical recipes for computational art and graphics

2. Wide coverage of topics including interactive art, computer vision, visualization, drawing in 3D, and much more with Processing

3. Create interactive art installations and learn to export your artwork for print, screen, Internet, and mobile devices

Please check **www.PacktPub.com** for information on our titles